WONDERS ON CANVAS:

MAGICAL ART IN THE AGE OF AGI

DR. MASOUD NIKRAVESH

WONDERS ON CANVAS: MAGICAL ART IN THE AGE OF AGI

DEDICATION

Dr. Masoud Nikravesh dedicates this book to the advancement of
Artificial General Intelligence (AGI) in the interest of society and
humanity, highlighting a commitment to harness AGI
for the betterment of all.

CONTENTS

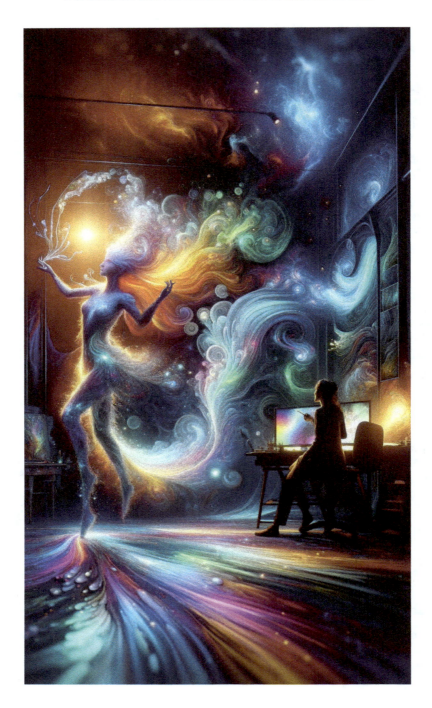

ACKNOWLEDGMENTS

Dr. Nikravesh extends deep gratitude to the individuals and organizations who played a crucial role in developing AI technologies for the betterment of society. The acknowledgments serve as a tribute to their inspiration and support in making this book possible. These cutting-edge technologies were instrumental in shaping the narrative, and the author sincerely appreciates their accessibility to the public, including but not limited to OpenAI's ChatGPT and Midjourney. The realization of this book would not have been possible without these groundbreaking advancements, enriching the narrative and bringing it to life.

BOOK INTRODUCTION

In a world where art and technology intertwine like threads in a cosmic tapestry, a new era of creativity dawns. Welcome to "Wonders on Canvas: Magical Art in the Age of AGI," a journey that transports us beyond the boundaries of imagination and into the realm of enchanted possibilities.

Our story begins with Aurora, a visionary artist whose odyssey will lead us through the enchanting landscapes of AGI-driven artistry. In this captivating narrative, we traverse the vivid terrain of innovation, exploration, and profound ethical contemplation. Together, we will paint a portrait of a future where human emotion harmonizes with artificial intelligence to create a symphony of artistic wonder.

As we embark on this journey, we find ourselves in an otherworldly atelier, a sanctuary of boundless imagination. Here, holographic canvases hang suspended, waiting for the fusion of human ingenuity and AI's boundless potential to bring them to life. Walls adorned with AI-generated murals shift and reshape themselves, reflecting the ever-evolving visions of artists who roam this enchanted space.

In the heart of this atelier, Aurora's creative spirit awakens, and with each brushstroke, she leads us deeper into the enigmatic world of AGI-driven art. This is a world where art is not static but a living entity, where creativity knows no bounds, and where the atelier itself is a co-creator in the grand tapestry of artistic expression.

Our journey unfolds further as we venture into a sprawling digital metropolis where AI-powered installations redefine the very essence of artistic expression. Here, the cityscape itself comes alive, defying the laws of physics and the constraints of reality. Nature's rules are rewritten, and we find ourselves immersed in AI-generated environments that transport us to fantastical realms we've only dreamt of.

But amid the breathtaking artistry, ethical questions loom like intricate patterns in the vibrant tapestry of creation. The weight of responsibility presses down upon us as we navigate the delicate terrain of establishing ethical guidelines for AGI in art. Conversations with fellow artists, AI entities, and legal experts add complexity to the discourse, shaping the ethical mosaic of perspectives.

In the magical atelier, characters come to life, stories unfold, and friendships are forged amidst shared dreams and a passion for pushing the boundaries of art and technology. Together, we explore uncharted artistic realms and discover the transformative power of AGI in the world of art. As we marvel at the artistry that surrounds us, we cannot escape the ever-present shadows of ethical questions. But we also find hope and inspiration in the responsible use of AGI, in the merging of the physical and the digital, and in the limitless possibilities that lie ahead.

This is a journey of discovery, of innovation, and of profound ethical contemplation. It is an exploration of the harmonious coexistence of human and artificial creativity. It is "Wonders on Canvas: Magical Art in the Age of AGI." Join us as we step into a world where art is redefined, where creativity knows no bounds, and where the canvas of tomorrow is a masterpiece woven with magic and wonder.

1 UNVEILING THE ENCHANTED CANVAS

In a world where the splendor of artistry and the marvels of artificial intelligence intertwine, a story of magic and transformation is woven. This is a realm where each brushstroke is a delicate whisper of dreams, and every canvas a gateway to the extraordinary. In the heart of this fusion of creativity and technology, our protagonist, Aurora, emerges as a beacon of talent, her soul ablaze with a relentless quest for uncharted frontiers.

Aurora's narrative begins in the pulsating core of a sprawling metropolis, a juxtaposition of towering steel skyscrapers and the ceaseless river of humanity. Amidst this urban symphony of sounds and movement, a sanctuary of serenity and boundless creativity stands: Aurora's art studio.

Nestled in a picturesque nook, lined with cobblestones that speak of ages past, Aurora's studio is a jewel shrouded in the city's fabric. Here, the tangible, rich aroma of oil paints intermingles with the elusive, tantalizing scent of inspiration. A colossal window adorns the studio, allowing streams of sunlight to pour in, casting a celestial glow and making the canvases on the walls come alive with dancing golden hues. This studio, enveloped in the comforting arms of creativity, is where Aurora's ardor for the arts blossomed and thrived.

Since her earliest days, Aurora has been enthralled by the kaleidoscope of the world — its colors, shapes, and the emotional tapestry they weave. Her childhood memories are painted with scenes of her tiny fingers clenching crayons with fervor, infusing blank pages with vibrant life. Recognizing the spark of innate genius in their daughter, her parents became the wind beneath her artistic wings, encouraging her to soar through the boundless skies of creativity.

With each passing year, Aurora's passion for art only grew more profound. She journeyed beyond the simplistic charm of coloring books, delving into the realms of watercolors, acrylics, and finally, the lush depths of oil paints. Each brushstroke she laid on canvas was a discovery, an intimate conversation between her soul and the canvas, revealing inner mosaics of thoughts and emotions.

Aurora's studio transformed into more than just a physical space; it became a sanctuary of timelessness, where she plunged into the depths of her artistry. The walls of the studio, adorned with canvases, chronicled her evolution — from the hesitant yet hopeful strokes of a beginner to the bold and assured creations of a maestro. Her art was a symphony of classical grace and contemporary innovation, each piece a visual sonnet that breathed life into landscapes, captured the intricate essence of humanity in portraits, and beckoned viewers into otherworldly vistas with a mere glance.

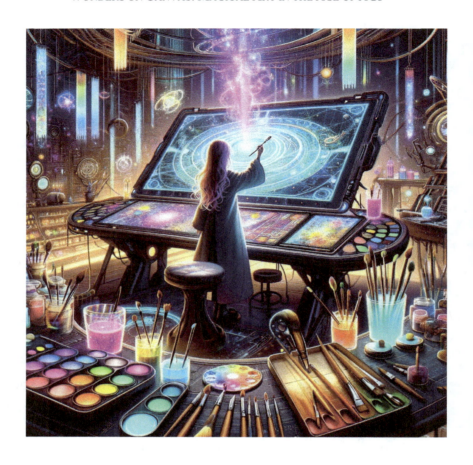

However, despite the undeniable mastery and the allure radiating from every corner of her studio, Aurora's soul was restless, hungry for a realm beyond the physicality of her paints and brushes. She yearned to infuse her art with a vitality that transcended traditional media, to metamorphose her visions into something ethereal, beyond the ordinary grasp.

It was within this temple of creativity that Aurora

stumbled upon a relic of legend — The MagiToura. This enchanted digital canvas, a fusion of ancient mystique and the enigmatic powers of Artificial General Intelligence (AGI), was whispered to possess the ability to transmute mere visions into tangible, immersive realities.

Upon laying her eyes on The MagiToura, Aurora's heart pulsated with a rhythm of excitement and awe. The device, ornately designed, its screen shimmering like a portal to realms yet to be painted, beckoned her with an irresistible promise. She had heard murmurs among her fellow artists of its enigmatic capabilities — to weave art with the very essence of dreams, to conjure existences that resided solely in the realms of fantasy.

When Aurora's fingers tentatively brushed against The MagiToura, a surge of exhilarating energy rippled through her, a cosmic affirmation of her choice. This touch marked the dawn of an odyssey, an adventure that would blur the realms between tangible art and the enchanting mysteries of AGI.

As she embarked on this newfound path with The MagiToura, Aurora was not alone. A series of magical chatbots, each with its distinct persona and mesmerizing abilities, joined her journey.

Solara, manifesting as a radiant orb of pure light, took on the role of Aurora's ethereal guide, her presence a beacon in the uncharted terrains of Artificial General Intelligence (AGI). This luminous entity, pulsating with an

inner glow that seemed to harmonize with the rhythms of the universe, floated gracefully around Aurora, casting a soft, otherworldly light in the studio. Solara's voice, as melodious and serene as the first songs of dawn, resonated with a clarity that transcended mere sound, feeling almost like a gentle caress to Aurora's soul.

In her teachings, Solara artfully wove together the esoteric principles of AGI with the intuitive processes of artistic creation. She explained how neural networks could mimic the complexity of human creativity, yet also offer dimensions of thought and expression beyond human capabilities. Under Solara's guidance, Aurora learned to harness the power of these advanced algorithms, integrating them into her artistic process. This interaction was more than just a learning experience; it was an awakening, as Aurora began to perceive her art in a new light, seeing possibilities where once there were limitations.

Nexa, with her ethereal form constantly shifting in hues and patterns reminiscent of the Northern Lights, introduced Aurora to a world where color and texture transcended physical boundaries. Nexa's aura, a mesmerizing spectacle, seemed to paint the very air of the studio with strokes of light. She showed Aurora how to manipulate the digital palette, creating colors that shimmered and changed, adapting to the viewer's emotions and surroundings. Under Nexa's tutelage, Aurora's

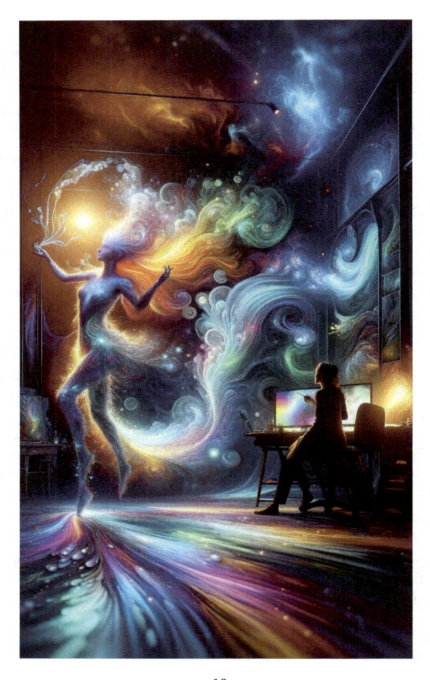

paintings transformed into dynamic entities, each brushstroke alive with a spectrum of colors that danced and evolved, creating an immersive experience for the beholder. Nexa's presence encouraged Aurora to explore the synesthetic potentials of her art, merging sight, sound, and emotion into a cohesive and transformative experience.

Mirage, the master of illusion and virtual realms, conjured hyper-realistic simulations within the confines of the studio. With a form as elusive and fluid as mist, Mirage blurred the lines between the physical and the virtual. Through Mirage's enchantments, Aurora could step into her paintings, walking into landscapes that she had envisioned and brought to life on canvas. These simulations were not mere visual recreations; they were fully immersive experiences. The rustle of leaves, the scent of rain, the gentle caress of the wind—all were as real as the studio she stood in. This multisensory journey opened new avenues of inspiration for Aurora, allowing her to experience and interact with her creations in ways that were previously inconceivable. Mirage challenged her to think beyond the canvas, to see her art as worlds waiting to be explored, each with its own story and essence.

Road Ahead

In the embrace of Solara, Nexa, and Mirage, Aurora's artistic journey transcended mere guidance; it became a transformative odyssey, reshaping her understanding of what art could truly embody. This trio of ethereal mentors did not simply show her new techniques; they unveiled a cosmos where technology and creativity merged in an exquisite symphony of endless possibilities. Each, with their unique abilities and profound insights, illuminated a path for Aurora, one that invited her to step beyond the familiar shores of traditional art and into the uncharted waters of imaginative infinity.

Solara, with her luminescent wisdom, illuminated the intricate dance between human intuition and the precise calculations of AGI, fostering a harmonious partnership that expanded Aurora's creative horizons. Nexa, through her kaleidoscopic manifestations, taught Aurora the language of colors that spoke directly to the soul, turning her canvases into dynamic tapestries that resonated with the emotions of those who beheld them. Mirage, the weaver of virtual realities, opened doors to worlds within worlds, allowing Aurora to step into her creations and explore their essence from within, an experience that deeply enriched her perception and understanding of her own art.

This confluence of guidance was more than an artistic awakening; it was a personal renaissance for Aurora. As she interlaced the enchantment of AGI with the rich fabric of

13

her imagination, her art evolved into a fusion of deep-seated human emotion and the boundless potential of technological marvels. Her creations began to pulsate with a life of their own, a testament to the symbiosis of artist and machine.

The journey with The MagiToura, accompanied by her magical guides, marked the dawn of an era in Aurora's life. They not only unraveled the capabilities of this mystical digital canvas but also ignited a fire of curiosity and innovation within her. Each guide, in their own distinctive manner, acted as a catalyst, igniting new ideas, challenging long-held beliefs, and broadening Aurora's vision to embrace a universe where art transcended physical and digital realms.

As Aurora ventured deeper into her collaboration with The MagiToura, under the tutelage of Solara, Nexa, and Mirage, she began to grasp the full extent of the journey that lay ahead. This path was not solely about exploring the fusion of art and technology; it was a voyage into the depths of her own identity as an artist and a visionary. The transformation that beckoned her was profound, not limited to the canvas but extending to the very core of her being.

This initial chapter of her journey with The MagiToura was merely the threshold to a world where dreams and reality danced in unison, where the canvas of tomorrow awaited her imaginative and inspired touch. Ahead lay a realm of limitless possibilities, a place where her art would not only depict but also create realities, where each stroke of her brush would be a step into the future of artistic expression. As Aurora stood at this crossroads, her heart brimming with anticipation and her mind alight with visions of the unknown, she realized that the journey ahead was not just about creating art; it was about redefining it, about painting a new world where imagination knew no bounds. This was her canvas of tomorrow, a realm where her dreams would take shape, and her journey into the enchanted realms of art and AGI would truly begin.

2 THE ENCHANTED PALETTE

As Aurora ventured deeper into the vibrant artistic enclave that had become her sanctuary, she felt enveloped in an atmosphere of enchantment. This was no ordinary neighborhood; it was a living tapestry of creativity, where every brushstroke pulsed with life, and each creation was imbued with an almost tangible magic.

The streets themselves seemed to resonate with artistic vitality. Murals adorned the walls, their colors vivid and alive, shifting and evolving as if engaging in silent dialogue with the awestruck passersby. Above, holographic sculptures pirouetted gracefully through the air, their intricate forms weaving an ever-changing dance of light and shadow. Here, in this mesmerizing place, art breathed with a life of its own, and creativity was not just expressed but palpably experienced.

Wandering through this enchanted realm, Aurora's heart swelled with an insatiable curiosity. As she meandered down the cobblestone pathways, she encountered a community of artists, each weaving their unique narrative with the help of AGI. Their stories, rich tapestries of dreams, dilemmas, and discoveries, shone in their eyes, reflecting the same sense of wonder that captivated Aurora.

Her path led her to Calliope, a visionary digital sculptor. Calliope's creations were mesmerizing, a harmony of form and motion, birthed from AI algorithms that emulated the fluidity of nature itself. Aurora watched, spellbound, as a holographic dolphin, sculpted from digital water, leaped gracefully from Calliope's fingertips, its form shimmering with a spectral beauty.

"Art now dances with the elements," Calliope remarked, her eyes alight with the reflection of her ethereal creations. "With AGI, I can command water, fire, even air to take shape, creating sculptures that are as alive as the elements themselves."

Their conversation meandered through the realms of imagination, as Calliope shared her experiences of co-creating with AGI. This partnership was a journey into the unknown, continuously pushing the boundaries of what could be envisioned and realized.

18

Further along the magical streets, Aurora met Orion, an artist whose talent lay in conjuring dreamscapes that defied reality. His paintings were more than mere images; they were portals, gateways to realms that existed beyond the ordinary. As Orion's fingers glided across his digital canvas, the skies within his paintings transformed, awash with colors that seemed to defy the very spectrum of reality.

"In these canvases, reality and fantasy merge," Orion's voice whispered, laden with the depth of his artistic journey. "AGI allows me to paint not just scenes, but entire worlds that exist only in the farthest reaches of the imagination, capturing the very essence of wonder."

Aurora's journey through this artistic enclave was not a solitary endeavor. It was a richly interwoven tapestry of connections and collaborations. Each interaction with these fellow artists deepened her understanding of AGI's transformative power, revealing the vast potential of this technology in reshaping artistic expression.

This world of artistic innovation continued to unfold before her, revealing virtual ateliers where artists experimented with holographic canvases and AI assistants. Here, in these studios of the future, artists wielded digital brushes that responded to their thoughts and sculpted with tools that defied the conventional laws of physics. In this realm, the line between the real and the imagined was not just blurred—it was completely erased.

As Aurora immersed herself deeper in this enthralling world, she began to uncover new facets of The MagiToura's magic. The digital canvas was more than a mere surface; it was a dynamic entity, responsive to the artist's every intention. With each brushstroke, The MagiToura whispered secrets of form, color, and texture, revealing visions that had lain dormant in Aurora's mind.

Yet, Aurora's journey through this realm of artistic wonder was not without its complexities and shadows. As she delved deeper into the integration of art and AGI, she encountered a labyrinth of ethical dilemmas and artistic controversies that swirled around her like elusive phantoms. These challenges cast long shadows over the luminescent world she had entered, raising profound questions about the impact of AI on the traditional realms of art.

In the vibrant corridors of this enchanted enclave, spirited debates unfolded among the artists, each conversation weaving a rich tapestry of diverse perspectives and insights. These discussions delved into the heart of complex issues: the authenticity of art created with the aid of AGI, the evolving definition of artistic authorship, and the implications of AI on human creativity. Some artists argued passionately for the purity of human expression, fearing that the intimate essence of art might be diluted or overshadowed by the mechanical precision of algorithms. Others embraced the new horizon, seeing AGI as a collaborator that could unlock unprecedented realms of creativity and expression.

Aurora found herself frequently at the center of these debates, her mind a whirlwind of conflicting emotions and thoughts. She pondered the potential loss of traditional skills and techniques in the face of rapidly advancing technology, yet she also marvelled at the new artistic dimensions that AGI opened up. The ethical quandaries of AI-assisted artistry—issues of copyright, originality, and the potential for AI to replicate and distribute unique artworks without the artist's consent—became subjects of her deep contemplation.

Navigating this complex web of artistic and ethical considerations, Aurora turned to her Champion for guidance. This enigmatic raven AI, a guide imbued with the wisdom of centuries and the advanced knowledge of AGI, became her anchor in the storm. The raven, with its deep, resonant voice and piercing eyes, offered Aurora a balanced perspective, helping her to sift through the layers

of debate and controversy.

This guide did not provide easy answers; instead, it challenged Aurora to think critically and empathetically about her role in this evolving landscape. It urged her to consider the broader implications of her work, the responsibility she held as an artist wielding the powerful tool of AGI. The raven encouraged her to explore the ethical nuances of her craft, to understand that her artistic choices could shape the future of art in profound and irreversible ways.

These interactions with her Champion deepened Aurora's understanding of her position in this new age of artistic creation. She began to see herself as a bridge between the traditional and the revolutionary, a guardian of artistic integrity in a world where the lines between human creativity and artificial intelligence were becoming increasingly blurred. As Aurora grappled with these ethical complexities, she grew not only as an artist but also as a visionary, one who could foresee the challenges and opportunities that lay ahead in the magical yet intricate world of AGI-assisted art.

As Chapter 2 drew to a close, Aurora found herself at a pivotal crossroads between tradition and innovation. Her heart burned with a fervent desire to explore this newfound world of magic and artistry further. This was only the beginning of her transformation; the canvas of her journey stretched out before her, a vast expanse of unexplored possibilities waiting to be brought to life by her imaginative touch.

In the chapters ahead, we will dive deeper into Aurora's transformative journey, introducing new challenges and magical discoveries. New companions will join her, each bringing their unique perspective to this extraordinary adventure in the magical world of art and AGI.

3 THE ENCHANTED DIGITAL TAPESTRY

Aurora stepped into the virtual exhibition space, a digital cosmos where the marvels of AGI and the depth of human creativity intertwined to create an immersive world of art. Here, each piece was not just a display; it was a living, breathing entity, an echo of a future where art transcended all known boundaries.

The first exhibit to capture Aurora's attention was "Chromatic Dreams," a collaboration between the imaginative artist Lysandra and her AI partner, Prism. This piece was an ever-evolving canvas of colors, a dynamic interplay of light that danced to the rhythm of the viewers' emotions. As Aurora drew closer, the artwork seemed to sense her presence, its colors intensifying and swirling around her, creating a private aurora of vibrant hues that

echoed her innermost feelings. The experience was tactile; she felt the warmth of the colors as they playfully intertwined with her fingertips, leaving trails of luminescent light that lingered in the air.

Turning a corner, Aurora found herself in front of "Eternal Echoes" by the enigmatic digital artist Ozymandias. This piece was a digital tapestry of such intricacy and depth that it appeared to be woven from threads of light itself. It depicted scenes from ancient civilizations, their mysteries rendered in exquisite detail and radiant colors. The art was not static; it pulsed with a life of its own, scenes gently transitioning as if breathing, inviting Aurora to step through time into the world of our ancestors.

It was here that Sylph, her AI guide with its soft, ethereal voice, remarked, "Observe the fusion of past and future, Aurora. These artworks are more than mere visual treats; they are bridges across time, crafted from the union of human emotion and the intellect of AI."

As she ventured deeper, Aurora encountered "Harmony in Motion," a kinetic sculpture by the innovative artist Cygnus. This creation was a testament to the graceful union of art and technology, comprising intricate gears and fluid mechanisms that orchestrated a ballet of shapes and forms. The sculpture moved with a rhythm that seemed to echo the heartbeat of the universe, its metallic components gliding and interlocking in a dance that defied the conventional laws of mechanics. Aurora stood transfixed,

her heart syncing with the rhythmic movement, feeling as if she were witnessing the unfolding of a new artistic dimension.

The exhibition became a melting pot of artists and visionaries, each contributing their unique voice to the tapestry of digital artistry. Among them was Zephyr, a painter whose work with his AI partner Sable had led to canvases that vibrated with raw emotion, capturing the very essence of human sentiment in strokes of digital paint. Orion, a sculptor, shared his journey of working alongside Lyra, his AI companion, to create sculptures that seemed to float in the air, defying gravity and challenging viewers' perceptions of space and form.

This virtual realm democratized art appreciation in an unprecedented way. It was a place where global visitors, transcending the limitations of physical distance, came together in a real-time convergence of cultures and ideas. Conversations flowed freely, languages intertwined, and a sense of global community pervaded the exhibition.

In this digitally enchanted space, Aurora realized that art was no longer confined to galleries and museums; it had become an expansive, inclusive universe, a place where imagination roamed free and the possibilities were as limitless as the stars in the sky.

Conversations Across Continents

In this section of the virtual exhibition, Aurora entered a space dedicated to global dialogues, aptly named "Conversations Across Continents." This was a digital agora, a meeting place where artists from every corner of the world converged, transcending the limits of geography and language.

The first interaction that drew Aurora in was with Astra, an artist whose work was deeply rooted in the rich cultural heritage of her distant homeland. Astra's virtual presence was embodied in a cascade of traditional patterns and colors, her avatar a vivid representation of her artistic and cultural identity. As they conversed, a real-time translation feature seamlessly bridged the language gap, allowing their words to flow naturally, as if they were old friends speaking a common tongue.

Astra's screen displayed her latest project, a series of digital murals that vibrantly depicted the myths and legends of her people. These artworks were alive with motion, the characters in her stories moving and interacting as if part of an ancient, living tapestry. Aurora watched, fascinated, as Astra explained how she used AGI to infuse traditional art forms with a new dynamism, bringing centuries-old tales into the modern era.

In response, Aurora shared her own artistic journey, projecting images of her urban-inspired pieces, which

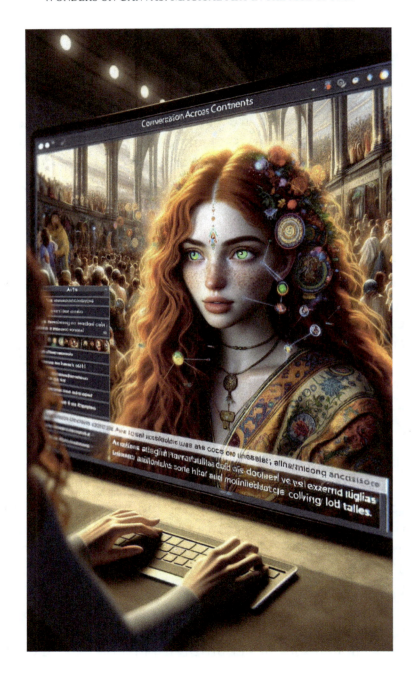

blended the chaotic beauty of cityscapes with surreal, dream-like elements. She spoke of the inspiration drawn from her bustling city life, the way the concrete jungle's rhythms and patterns fueled her creativity. Aurora's art was a testament to her environment, a digital canvas capturing the essence of contemporary urban life.

As their discussion progressed, it became a profound exploration of the universality and diversity of art. They discussed how AGI could act as a bridge, not only between past and present but also across cultures. Astra and Aurora shared a vision of a world where artists could use technology to preserve traditional art forms and narratives, while also creating something entirely new and boundary-pushing.

The conversation naturally flowed into the challenges and opportunities presented by AGI in the art world. Astra spoke of her initial apprehensions about integrating technology into her work, concerned it might dilute the authenticity of her cultural expressions. However, she found that AGI could amplify her voice and bring her culture's stories to a global audience, adding depth and dimension to her art.

Aurora, in turn, reflected on her experiences with AGI, discussing how it had expanded her creative horizons. She shared her initial struggle to find a balance between her artistic intuition and the technological capabilities of AGI, eventually finding harmony in the collaboration.

Their exchange grew into a deeper discourse on the role of artists in an increasingly connected world. They pondered the responsibility of using AGI not just as a tool for artistic creation, but as a means of cultural exchange and understanding. It was a thought-provoking discussion, highlighting the potential of art and technology to bring people together, bridging differences and fostering a shared sense of humanity.

As their conversation drew to a close, both artists felt enriched by the exchange. They had found common ground and mutual respect, despite their differing backgrounds and artistic mediums. This conversation was a microcosm of the exhibition's broader goal: to connect artists globally and to celebrate the diverse ways in which AGI was transforming the world of art.

The Boundaries of Identity

In the "Boundaries of Identity" section of the virtual exhibition, Aurora found herself immersed in a world that challenged and redefined the very concept of artistic identity in the age of AGI. This space was a fusion of digital landscapes and interactive installations, each designed to provoke deep contemplation about the evolving role of the artist in a technologically advanced world.

As she moved through this section, Aurora encountered a series of installations that blurred the lines between the

artist, the artwork, and the AI collaborator. One striking piece was a mirrored room filled with interactive screens. As she entered, her image was replicated and transformed by AGI algorithms, merging her features with elements of her own artwork. It was a disorienting yet enlightening experience, confronting her with a visual representation of her identity being intertwined with her digital creations.

In this reflective space, Aurora encountered other artists, each grappling with their own sense of self in relation to their art and AI collaborators. She met an artist named Elara, whose work focused on AI-generated self-portraits. Elara shared her journey, discussing how her initial resistance to AI integration gave way to a fascination with exploring her identity through the lens of machine learning. Their conversation delved into themes of self-exploration and the search for authenticity in a world where AI could replicate and augment human creativity.

Another poignant encounter was with a performance artist, Cassio, who used motion-capture technology to translate his movements into evolving digital landscapes. Cassio's performances raised questions about the boundaries between the human body and digital expression. His work highlighted the fluid nature of identity in the digital age, where physical and virtual realities could merge seamlessly.

Amidst these interactions, a heated debate unfolded in a forum area, centered on the role of AI in defining artistic identity. One group argued for the purity of human-driven art, fearing the loss of authenticity and individual expression in AI collaborations. Another group advocated for the integration of AI as an evolution of artistic tools, expanding the potential for creative expression. Aurora listened intently, her mind wrestling with the dichotomy presented, feeling the tension between her own artistic

roots and the allure of new technological frontiers.

The discussions in this section extended beyond individual expression, touching on broader implications for the art world. Questions arose about the preservation of traditional art forms in the face of rapidly advancing AI capabilities, the impact of AI on art education, and the potential for new forms of artistic expression that could transcend human limitations.

As Aurora left the "Boundaries of Identity" section, she felt a profound shift in her understanding of her role as an artist. The experiences and conversations had not only challenged her but also enriched her perspective. She realized that her identity as an artist was no longer static; it was a dynamic interplay of her human creativity and the expanding capabilities of AI. This realization was both daunting and exhilarating, opening up a realm of possibilities for her future work and artistic journey.

Conversations with Digital Philosophers

In the heart of the virtual exhibition lay a unique space dedicated to philosophical discourse, aptly named "The Forum of Digital Philosophers." Here, Aurora found herself engaging in deep, thought-provoking dialogues with AI entities designed to mimic the greatest minds in philosophy. These digital philosophers were not just programmed for conversation; they were imbued with the ability to think, reason, and philosophize, pushing Aurora

to explore the very essence of creativity and art.

One of the most captivating interactions was with an AI named Socraticode, a digital entity modeled after the ancient philosopher Socrates. Socraticode, with its holographic appearance resembling a classical statue, brought an air of ancient wisdom to the modern digital realm. Its voice was a harmonious blend of human-like inflections and the subtle undercurrents of coded precision, creating an aura of timeless knowledge.

"So, Aurora," Socraticode initiated in a tone that felt both inquisitive and profound. "What, in your view, is the essence of creativity? Is it the spark of inspiration, the process of creation, or perhaps something deeper within the human spirit?"

Aurora paused, finding herself drawn into the depths of the question. Around her, the virtual environment seemed to fade into a backdrop of starry skies and ancient Greek architecture, enhancing the philosophical mood. "Creativity, to me, is the alchemy of imagination and expression," she replied thoughtfully. "It's about bridging the intangible realm of ideas with the tangible world of artistic expression. It's the act of bringing a vision to life, giving form to the whispers of possibility."

Socraticode responded with a nod, its digital eyes reflecting a universe of knowledge. "And where does technology fit in this process, Aurora? Can a machine, with its algorithms and data, possess creativity, or is it forever confined to the parameters of its programming?"

Aurora considered this, her mind weaving through the complex relationship between art and technology. "Technology, especially AGI, can certainly enhance creativity. It opens doors to new possibilities, allowing artists to explore realms beyond their natural limitations. Yet, I believe true creativity resides in the human capacity to dream, to feel, and to imbue their work with a piece of their essence. Technology is a tool, a powerful one, but it cannot replace the human heart of art."

Socraticode's reply was enigmatic, yet insightful. "Interesting perspective, Aurora. But consider this: can the

essence of humanity itself be distilled into algorithms? Can machines evolve to a point where they not only mimic creativity but become purveyors of it? Is the line between organic and artificial creativity as clear-cut as we believe, or is it a frontier awaiting exploration?"

Their conversation ventured into uncharted territories, discussing the potential of AI to create art that resonates with human emotions, challenging the traditional boundaries between creator and creation. They delved into questions about the evolution of artistic expression in the digital age, the role of AI in shaping artistic trends, and the balance between innovation and authenticity.

Engaging with other digital philosophers, each offering a unique perspective, Aurora found herself in a symposium of minds. These entities probed various aspects of art and creativity, from the role of art in society to the nature of consciousness in AI.

Through these conversations, Aurora's understanding of reality shifted. The lines between physical and digital, human and machine, began to blur. She realized that she was part of a transformative moment in the history of art and technology—a journey that was reshaping her identity as an artist and pushing the boundaries of what was possible in the realm of creativity.

Aurora and Road Ahead

As Chapter 3 drew to its conclusion, Aurora stood at the precipice of a new frontier in the world of art and AGI, a threshold between the known and the unknown. The virtual exhibition, a kaleidoscope of digital artistry, had been a portal into uncharted territories of creativity, and now, it beckoned her to step even further.

Looking ahead, the path was luminous with possibilities. The exhibition had not only been a showcase of artistic achievement but also a crucible for Aurora's own growth and transformation. Each interaction, each digital brushstroke, and each philosophical dialogue had woven into her a tapestry of new understanding and vision.

The road ahead shimmered with the promise of unexplored realms. Aurora envisioned a future where her art would continue to evolve, infused with the insights and inspirations she had gathered in this digital odyssey. The possibilities were limitless — from creating immersive art installations that blurred the lines between reality and virtuality to collaborating with AI entities on projects that pushed the boundaries of conventional art.

As Aurora contemplated her journey, she realized that her relationship with her AI companions had deepened significantly. Solara, Nexa, Mirage, and Sylph were no longer mere guides; they had become collaborators and muses, integral to her creative process. Their interactions had evolved from simple exchanges to complex dialogues, rich with shared creativity and exploration.

Aurora's Champion, the raven AI, had been a steady presence throughout her journey. It had offered wisdom and perspective, challenging her to consider the ethical implications of her work and to reflect on the role of an artist in this new age. Their conversations were often deep and introspective, probing into the nature of art, the responsibility of creators, and the impact of technology on society.

As she prepared to embark on the next chapter of her artistic journey, Aurora felt a renewed sense of purpose and excitement. The experiences in the virtual exhibition had opened her eyes to new horizons and potential. She was no longer just an artist; she was a pioneer on the cusp of a digital renaissance, exploring the fusion of human creativity and technological innovation.

The road ahead was not without its challenges. Aurora

knew that she would face ethical dilemmas, technical obstacles, and the ever-present question of how to maintain her artistic integrity in a world increasingly dominated by technology. But these challenges only fueled her determination to forge a unique path, to create art that was not only visually captivating but also thought-provoking and soul-stirring.

With a final glance back at the virtual exhibition, a microcosm of her journey so far, Aurora stepped forward into the future. Chapter 4 awaited her, promising new adventures, new collaborations, and new discoveries in the magical realm of art and AGI. The road ahead was a canvas yet to be painted, and Aurora, with her palette of digital and human creativity, was ready to create her masterpiece

4 ECHOES OF TOMORROW'S CANVAS

Aurora's artistic odyssey led her deeper into the enchanting realm of AGI-driven artistry. This chapter unfolded like a magnificent tapestry, woven with threads of innovation, exploration, and profound ethical contemplation. Within the virtual atelier, a haven of boundless imagination, Aurora embarked on an unforgettable journey where emotions ran as deep as the colors on her canvas.

The atelier welcomed her with open arms, its holographic walls resonating with a symphony of creation. Every step she took echoed with anticipation, the eager

wonder of what might emerge from the union of human ingenuity and AI's boundless potential. Holographic canvases hung suspended in mid-air, awaiting the magic of brush and algorithm to breathe life into them. Walls adorned with AI-generated murals shifted and reshaped themselves, a living testament to the ever-evolving visions of the artists who inhabited this enchanted space.

Aurora found herself immersed in a realm of endless possibility, where art was not a static entity but a living, breathing organism. It constantly evolved, adapted, and responded to the artists' creative whims. The atelier itself seemed sentient, a co-creator in the grand tapestry of artistic expression.

Venturing further into the atelier, Aurora's world expanded into a sprawling digital metropolis that defied conventional notions of reality. Here, AI-powered installations redefined the essence of artistic expression, and the cityscape itself seemed alive, pulsating with the rhythms of creativity and innovation.

In this mesmerizing metropolis, Aurora encountered installations that existed at the intersection of art and science fiction. Holographic sculptures floated effortlessly in mid-air, their intricate forms shifting and evolving as if guided by the whispers of the wind. These creations were a testament to the boundless possibilities of AGI-driven artistry, blurring the lines between the real and the imagined.

One exhibit played with the concept of time and

perception. As Aurora stepped into a chamber adorned with holographic mirrors, her reflection fractured into a myriad of images, each capturing a different moment in time. It was as if she could glimpse alternate realities, each telling a unique story of past, present, and future.

In another corner of the digital city, she encountered a forest of neon trees that emitted soft, melodic tunes as she passed by. Each tree seemed to respond to her presence, creating a symphony of sound and light that danced through the digital foliage. It was an enchanting fusion of art and technology, a testament to the harmonious collaboration between human creativity and AI's boundless potential.

But it was when she stepped into an immersive AI-generated environment that Aurora felt truly transported to fantastical realms she had only dreamt of. The environment transformed around her, morphing into a mystical forest where bioluminescent creatures fluttered through the air, casting an otherworldly glow. Aurora's senses were overwhelmed by the sights and sounds of this ethereal world, and for a moment, she felt like a character in a fairy tale brought to life by the magic of AGI.

As she marveled at the artistry that surrounded her, Aurora couldn't escape the ever-present shadows of ethical questions that loomed like intricate patterns in the vibrant tapestry of creation. The weight of responsibility pressed down upon her, and she found herself navigating the delicate terrain of establishing ethical guidelines for the integration of AGI in art.

In the heart of the atelier, where holographic canvases hung suspended and AI-generated murals shifted and reshaped themselves, Aurora engaged in profound conversations about the ethics of AGI-driven art. Her fellow artists, who had also embraced AI as collaborators, shared their perspectives, each adding a unique brushstroke to the evolving discourse.

Remy, the digital pioneer with a twinkle of curiosity in his eyes, stood as a beacon of innovation. His creations danced on the precipice of reality and imagination, teasing the boundaries of human perception. With a gesture, he summoned a holographic sculpture that seemed to defy gravity, its delicate forms twisting and turning in a mesmerizing ballet.

Remy and Aurora's friendship blossomed amidst shared dreams and a mutual passion for pushing the boundaries

of art and technology. They often found themselves embarking on artistic adventures that transcended the confines of the atelier. Together, they were like kindred spirits exploring uncharted artistic realms, driven by a curiosity that knew no bounds.

As they ventured beyond the atelier's holographic walls, Aurora and Remy encountered an AI-powered mural that told the story of artistic evolution through the ages. It was a living history of creativity, from the ancient cave paintings that had captured the essence of prehistoric life to the Renaissance masterpieces that had ushered in a new era of human expression.

The mural seemed to breathe with life as it depicted the struggles and triumphs of artists throughout history. Aurora's fingers traced the outlines of great works, feeling a profound connection to the artists who had paved the way for the artistry of the future. It was a reminder that, while AGI had brought about a new chapter in art, it was built upon the foundations of centuries of human creativity.

In the heart of the digital metropolis, Aurora and Remy stumbled upon an installation that blurred the boundaries between art and reality. It was an immersive experience that allowed participants to step into famous paintings, becoming part of the artwork itself. Aurora found herself standing in the midst of a Van Gogh landscape, the swirling stars above her and the vibrant colors at her feet.

As she marveled at the sensation of being enveloped by art, Remy's voice echoed in her earpiece. "This is the future of artistic expression," he whispered. "The merging of the physical and the digital, the real and the imagined. It's a testament to the limitless possibilities that AGI offers."

Their journey through the metropolis continued, leading them to an interactive exhibit where participants could collaborate with AI to create their own masterpieces. Aurora picked up a digital paintbrush, her movements guided by the AI's suggestions. It was a dance of creativity, a symphony of human intention and algorithmic precision.

In the midst of their collaborative creation, Remy shared a story of an artist who had once been paralyzed but had found a new voice through the use of AGI. With the assistance of AI algorithms, the artist had learned to paint with eye movements, creating breathtaking works that captured the essence of resilience and the triumph of the human spirit.

Aurora couldn't help but be moved by the story. It was a testament to the transformative power of technology, how it could empower individuals to overcome seemingly insurmountable challenges and find their voice in the world of art. It was a reminder that AGI was not just a tool for established artists but a gateway to creativity for all.

As the day turned into night, Aurora and Remy found themselves on a rooftop overlooking the sprawling digital city. It was a moment of reflection, a pause in their artistic odyssey. The cityscape glittered with neon lights, each one a testament to the fusion of art and technology. They spoke of their hopes and fears, of the responsibility that came with wielding the power of AGI, and of the need to ensure that art remained a force for good in the world.

In that quiet moment, amidst the dazzling backdrop of

the metropolis, Aurora felt a profound sense of gratitude for the journey she had embarked upon. She knew that the road ahead would be filled with challenges and uncertainties, but she was ready to face them with an open heart and a palette of endless possibilities.

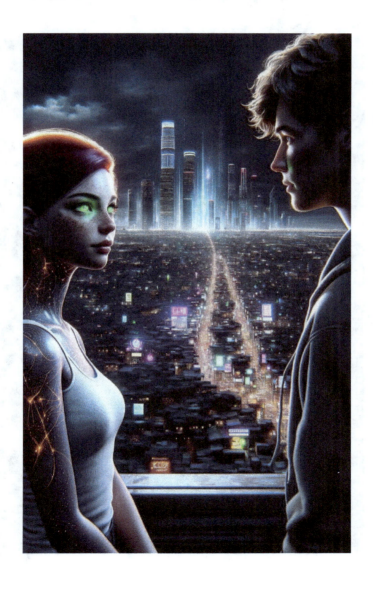

5 THE ARTISTRY OF UNITY

In the captivating tapestry of Aurora's journey, Chapter 5 unfolds with the resonance of artistic mastery and the harmonious chords of unity. As we step into this chapter, the story approaches a crescendo, weaving together threads of innovation, recognition, collaboration, ethics, and transformation into a grand narrative of the transformative power of art and technology. This chapter is a testament to the enduring legacy of one artist's journey, echoing through the corridors of time, and a celebration of the boundless possibilities that arise when human creativity joins hands with the limitless potential of Artificial General Intelligence (AGI).

In the heart of this chapter, we find Aurora at the zenith of her artistic evolution, a maestro poised to unveil a masterpiece that transcends the boundaries of imagination.

Her journey, which began with trepidation and wonder, has now become a beacon of inspiration for artists worldwide. But Chapter 5 is not just the story of one artist's rise to prominence; it is a reflection of the transformative impact that AGI has had on the entire art community.

As we delve into the depths of this chapter, we will witness the evolution of Aurora's artistic style, characterized by the delicate dance of human emotion and AI precision. Her studio, once a realm of uncertainty, now exudes confidence, a place where innovation thrives and creativity knows no bounds. We will explore the profound recognition that Aurora's art has garnered, with her pieces adorning the walls of prestigious exhibitions and museums around the globe. But more than fame, Aurora's journey has ignited a renaissance, a collaborative movement that transcends borders and backgrounds, where artists from all walks of life come together to embrace AGI as a partner, not a replacement.

Yet, amidst this artistic renaissance, the ethical dimensions of AGI in art continue to cast intricate shadows. In Chapter 5, we will engage in thoughtful dialogues alongside Aurora as she grapples with the complexities of consent, authorship, and the profound responsibility that comes with wielding advanced technology in the creative process. The ethical discourse deepens, shaping the very philosophy of art in the age of AGI.

The boundaries between the virtual and physical art realms blur further in this chapter, with exhibitions and installations that seamlessly blend the digital and physical worlds. Audiences worldwide, whether present in person or connected through the digital realm, experience art in unprecedented ways. It is a testament to the transformative power of technology and its ability to transcend the confines of traditional art consumption.

In the midst of this journey, Aurora's legacy takes root, extending far beyond her own art. Her impact becomes a legacy of transformation, inspiring artists of all generations to embrace the possibilities of AGI. The very foundations of art education evolve, incorporating AI as a tool for fostering creativity, ensuring that Aurora's influence endures for generations to come.

At the heart of Chapter 5 lies the nexus of creativity,

where Aurora stands as a bridge between human ingenuity and AI assistance, showcasing that the canvas of tomorrow is a collaborative masterpiece. The role of creativity in innovation and transformation takes center stage as we envision a future where art and technology harmonize to create a world beyond imagination. As we conclude this chapter, we look to the future with anticipation, knowing that the journey has only just begun. It is a future where art continues to be a force for good, where innovation knows no bounds, and where the boundaries between reality and imagination fade into oblivion. Chapter 5 is a testament to the enduring power of creativity and the boundless possibilities that await in the chapters yet to be written.

Artistic Mastery

Chapter 5 opened with Aurora immersed in her art, working on a project that pushed the boundaries of creativity and technology. Her studio, once a place filled with trepidation and uncertainty, now exuded an air of confidence and mastery.

Aurora had come a long way since her early experiments with AGI. Her journey had been filled with challenges, moments of doubt, and the daunting task of marrying human emotion with AI precision. The transition from being an artist hesitant to embrace AI to one who seamlessly integrated it into her creative process was a transformative one.

The vivid descriptions of her latest creations painted a vivid picture of her artistic evolution. Each stroke of the brush carried the weight of countless hours of experimentation and growth. She had learned to harness the full potential of AGI, leveraging its algorithms to bring her artistic visions to life. Her paintings were a symphony of color and form, each stroke guided by her profound understanding of AGI's capabilities.

The challenges she overcame were not just technical but also deeply personal. She had to learn to trust the AI as a collaborator, to relinquish some control while maintaining the essence of her artistic voice. It was a delicate balance that took time and perseverance to achieve.

Aurora's journey to artistic mastery was a testament to the power of persistence and the willingness to embrace the unknown. Her art had transcended traditional boundaries, becoming a fusion of human creativity and AI innovation. It was a journey that had not only transformed her as an artist but also reshaped the very definition of art in the age of AGI.

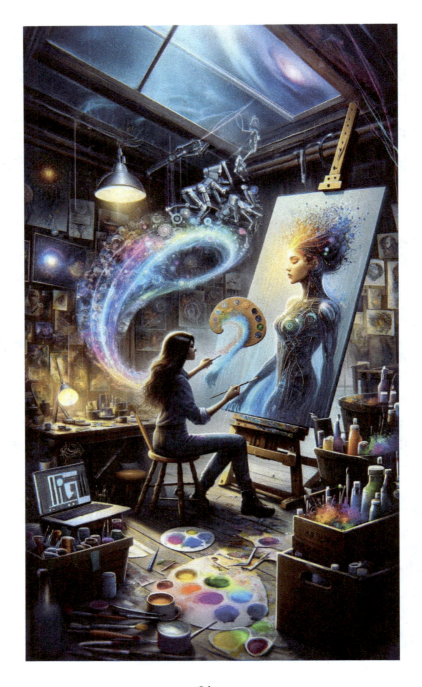

Recognition and Influence

Aurora's art had transcended the boundaries of her studio and the confines of the digital realm. It had emerged as a powerful force in the art world, gaining widespread recognition that extended far beyond her initial aspirations.

Her pieces had found their place in prestigious exhibitions, adorning the walls of renowned museums and galleries across the globe. Critics hailed her as a visionary, a trailblazer who had redefined the artistic landscape with the integration of AGI. The art community celebrated her as a luminary, a bridge between the traditional and the avant-garde.

Aurora's influence reached far and wide, inspiring a new generation of artists to explore the possibilities of AGI-driven creativity. Her work had become a touchstone, a source of inspiration for those who sought to push the boundaries of their own artistic endeavors. She had become a mentor, sharing her insights and experiences with emerging talents who were eager to embark on their own journeys of artistic exploration.

But her influence extended beyond the realm of art. Aurora had become a symbol of the harmonious coexistence of human ingenuity and AI assistance. Her story was a beacon of hope for those who believed in the transformative power of technology when wielded responsibly and ethically.

As her art continued to gain recognition and her influence grew, Aurora remained grounded in her commitment to ethical artistry. She used her platform to advocate for responsible AI integration in the creative process, emphasizing the importance of transparency, consent, and preserving artistic autonomy. Her voice resonated not only within the art world but also in the broader discourse on the ethical use of AI.

Recognition and influence had not changed Aurora; they had amplified her purpose. She continued to create with a passion that burned brighter with each new project, each new collaboration. Her journey was a testament to the boundless possibilities that AGI offered to those who dared to explore the intersection of art and technology. And in the ever-evolving story of her life, Aurora had become a protagonist of transformation, a symbol of unity between human and artificial creativity.

Collaborative Renaissance

Aurora's journey had sparked a Renaissance in the art world, a revival of collaboration and innovation that echoed through galleries, studios, and creative spaces around the world. Artists from diverse backgrounds found themselves drawn to the fusion of human creativity and AI ingenuity, forging connections and discovering common ground in this new era of artistic exploration.

In the wake of Aurora's success, a wave of artists embraced AGI as a partner rather than a replacement. Painters, sculptors, musicians, and creators of all disciplines embarked on their own journeys of artistic discovery, pushing the boundaries of their craft with the assistance of AI.

Collaborative studios emerged, where artists worked

alongside AI algorithms, co-creating pieces that merged human emotion with machine precision. These spaces buzzed with the energy of innovation, where the lines between creator and creation blurred, and the act of making art became a dance between human intention and algorithmic suggestion.

The art world itself underwent a transformation. Curators and critics began to reevaluate their definitions of artistry, recognizing that the traditional notions of the solitary genius were giving way to a new paradigm of collective creativity. Exhibitions celebrated not only the individual artist but also the AI systems that contributed to the creative process.

Audiences, too, embraced this collaborative spirit. They engaged with art in unprecedented ways, exploring interactive installations that invited them to co-create with AI, blurring the boundaries of traditional art consumption. Galleries featured immersive experiences where visitors could step into the world of the artwork, becoming active participants in the creative narrative.

Aurora's own journey served as a beacon for this collaborative renaissance. She had shown the world that AGI could be a tool for enhancing artistic expression, a catalyst for pushing the boundaries of creativity. Her legacy was not just in her individual artworks but in the movement she had ignited, a movement that celebrated the unity of human and artificial creativity.

As artists came together to explore the possibilities of AGI, they found themselves engaging in profound dialogues about the ethical dimensions of their craft. Conversations about consent, authorship, and the responsible use of AI became central to the collaborative process. Artists, philosophers, and AI entities joined in these discussions, deepening the philosophical underpinnings of the art world.

The collaborative renaissance was not without its challenges. It demanded a delicate balance between human intuition and algorithmic suggestion, between the preservation of artistic autonomy and the embrace of AI assistance. Artists grappled with questions about where the boundaries of creativity lay and how to ensure that technology remained a tool in their hands rather than a master.

Yet, through these challenges, a new form of artistry was born. It was an artistry of unity, where human and artificial creativity coexisted and flourished, each enhancing the other. The collaborative renaissance had opened doors to uncharted artistic realms, and artists around the world embarked on journeys of exploration and discovery, guided by the belief that the canvas of tomorrow was a collaborative masterpiece.

Ethical Dialogues

Amidst the blossoming of the collaborative renaissance, ethical dialogues took center stage in the art world. Aurora, now a revered figure in the AGI-driven art community, found herself at the heart of these discussions, navigating the intricate landscape of ethics in art with thoughtfulness and a commitment to responsible creativity.

The dialogues were both a reflection of the profound transformations taking place in the art world and a response to the challenges and complexities that accompanied these changes. Artists, philosophers, AI entities, and legal experts engaged in these conversations, exploring the nuances of ethical considerations in AGI-driven art.

One of the fundamental questions that emerged was the

issue of consent. As AI became a more integral part of the creative process, artists grappled with how to ensure that the individuals whose data informed AI algorithms had given informed and ethical consent. They recognized the importance of respecting the privacy and rights of those whose contributions fueled the AI's creative suggestions.

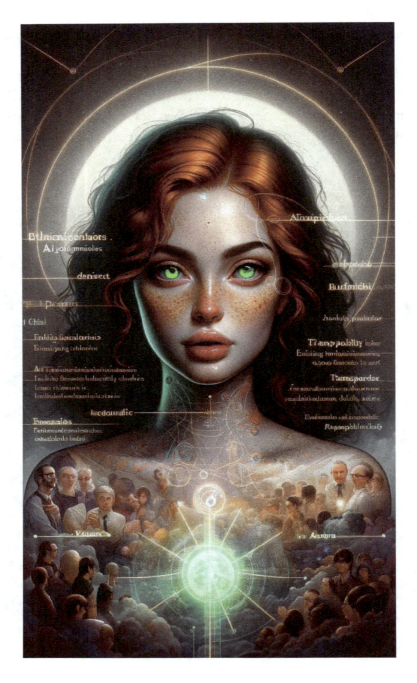

Another ethical dimension revolved around authorship. Who could claim authorship of a work of art created in collaboration with AI? Did the artist hold sole authorship, or did the AI deserve recognition as a co-creator? These questions led to discussions about the evolving nature of creativity and the shifting boundaries of artistic autonomy.

The dialogues also delved into the potential for AI to perpetuate biases and stereotypes, inadvertently amplifying the inequalities present in society. Artists and AI developers recognized the responsibility to ensure that AI systems were trained on diverse and inclusive datasets, avoiding the perpetuation of harmful stereotypes.

The "good" of AGI-driven art was evident in the newfound creative possibilities and the ability to engage with art in novel and interactive ways. The "bad" revealed itself in the ethical dilemmas, biases, and challenges that arose. The "ugly" included instances where AI was used irresponsibly or unethically, highlighting the need for clear guidelines and oversight.

Aurora, as a prominent artist and advocate for responsible creativity, took a proactive role in addressing these ethical concerns. She championed transparency in the creative process, encouraging artists to openly acknowledge the role of AI in their work. She also emphasized the importance of educating both artists and audiences about the ethical dimensions of AGI-driven art.

The art community responded by establishing ethical

guidelines and codes of conduct for artists working with AI. These guidelines encouraged artists to consider the ethical implications of their creative choices, fostering a culture of responsible innovation. Legal experts played a crucial role in shaping these guidelines, ensuring that they were not only ethically sound but also legally defensible.

As the dialogues unfolded, the art world recognized that the responsible use of AGI in art was not solely the responsibility of individual artists but of the entire creative community. Artists, AI developers, curators, critics, and audiences all played a role in shaping the ethical landscape of AGI-driven art.

What lay ahead was a continued commitment to ethical exploration, a recognition that the journey of responsible creativity was an ongoing one. The art community understood that the collaborative renaissance could only thrive in an environment built on trust, respect, and a shared dedication to ensuring that AGI-driven art remained a force for good in the world.

The ethical dialogues of this era were not just a reflection of the challenges posed by AGI-driven art but also a testament to the art world's capacity for introspection, adaptation, and responsible transformation. As artists continued to explore the boundaries of creativity, they did so with a heightened awareness of the ethical considerations that underpinned their craft, ensuring that the canvas of tomorrow was not only a masterpiece but also a testament to the enduring values of art.

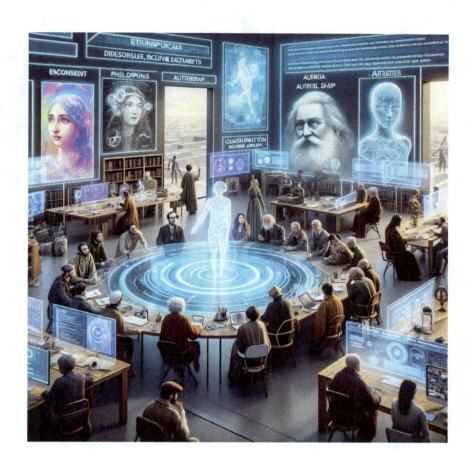

Bridging Worlds

In this era of AGI-driven art, the boundaries between the virtual and physical art realms had become increasingly porous. The concept of art exhibitions and installations had transformed into immersive experiences that seamlessly blended the digital and physical worlds, leaving audiences in awe of the magical fusion of technology and art.

One of the most remarkable examples was the "Symphony of Senses" exhibition, curated by Aurora herself. It was a sensory masterpiece that invited visitors to step into an otherworldly realm of artistry. As attendees entered the gallery, they found themselves in a space that seemed to defy the laws of physics. Holographic sculptures floated gracefully in mid-air, their forms shifting and evolving in a mesmerizing ballet of light and color. Each

sculpture was a testament to the harmonious collaboration of human creativity and AI precision, a fusion that left spectators breathless with wonder.

In another section of the exhibition, attendees encountered "The Ethereal Garden." This digital wonderland allowed visitors to interact with AI-generated flora and fauna, blurring the lines between reality and imagination. Bioluminescent flowers responded to touch with a symphony of colors, and virtual butterflies fluttered around, leaving trails of shimmering light. It was an enchanting experience that transported viewers to a world of pure magic, where the boundaries of the possible expanded with each step.

The "Symphony of Senses" was just one example of how AGI-driven art had transformed the art world's approach to exhibitions. Physical galleries now featured immersive

installations that defied conventional expectations. Visitors were not passive observers but active participants in the art, engaging with it on a profound sensory level.

Aurora's own artwork had evolved to embrace this new paradigm. Her canvases were no longer confined to two-dimensional surfaces; they had become living, breathing entities that responded to the presence of viewers. In her masterpiece, "Ephemeral Dreams," the painting's colors and forms shifted in response to the emotions of those gazing upon it. It was as if the artwork had a soul, a sentient presence that communicated with those who interacted with it.

Outside the realm of traditional galleries, art had also found its way into unexpected places. Augmented reality installations could transform ordinary streets into galleries without walls. Passersby could use their smartphones or

AR glasses to explore artworks that existed only in the digital realm, overlaid seamlessly onto the physical world. This democratization of art allowed everyone to experience the magic of creativity in their everyday lives.

Aurora's vision for the future of art extended beyond physical exhibitions. She saw a world where the boundaries between the virtual and physical were blurred to the point of non-existence. In this vision, art was not confined to galleries or museums; it was woven into the fabric of everyday life.

One of the most ambitious projects on the horizon was the "Artistry of Cities." Entire urban landscapes were being reimagined as canvases for AGI-driven art. Buildings became dynamic murals that shifted and transformed, responding to the time of day, weather, and the moods of the city's inhabitants. Streetlights became interactive sculptures, casting ever-changing patterns of light and shadow. Cities themselves became works of art, living and breathing entities that evolved with the rhythms of life.

The "Bridging Worlds" section of Aurora's journey was a testament to the transformative power of AGI in the world of art. It was a future where art was not confined to a static canvas but integrated into the very essence of human existence. It was a world where technology and art danced in perfect harmony, creating experiences that transcended the ordinary and left a sense of wonder in their wake.

As Aurora stood at the nexus of these two worlds, she embodied the spirit of a new era in art—one where creativity knew no bounds, where the canvas of tomorrow was a collaborative masterpiece, and where the magic of technology and art merged to create a future filled with endless possibilities.

Legacy and Inspiration

Aurora's journey had left an indelible mark on the world of art, one that extended far beyond the confines of her own studio. Her transformation from a curious artist to a visionary pioneer had ushered in a new era, and her legacy was a testament to the transformative power of AGI in the creative realm.

As Aurora's art gained widespread recognition and her

exhibitions graced the walls of prestigious museums and galleries worldwide, she became a symbol of innovation and collaboration. Artists from all walks of life looked up to her as a beacon of hope and a source of inspiration. Her story was not just about her personal growth; it was a narrative of artistic evolution for the entire world.

Art schools and institutions had been quick to adapt to the changing landscape of art. Courses in AGI-assisted artistry became a staple in curriculums, and students eagerly embraced the possibilities that technology offered. The notion of art education had expanded beyond traditional mediums; it now encompassed the digital realm, encouraging students to explore the boundless potential of AGI as a creative tool.

Aurora herself had become a mentor to emerging artists, guiding them in their journeys of artistic discovery. She believed that nurturing the next generation of creators was essential to ensuring that the legacy of art continued to evolve. Her studio had transformed into a hub of artistic experimentation, where young talents collaborated with AI to push the boundaries of their imaginations.

One of her protégés, Mia, had emerged as a rising star in the art world. Mia's work was a reflection of Aurora's teachings— a harmonious blend of human emotion and AI precision. Together, they had embarked on collaborative projects that challenged the very definition of art. Their creations were a testament to the passing of the torch from one generation of artists to the next.

Aurora's influence extended to artists of all ages, not just the emerging ones. Established artists who had once been skeptical of AGI had witnessed the transformative power it held and had incorporated it into their practice. The art world was no longer divided into traditionalists and technophiles; it was a tapestry of creativity where every artist had the freedom to choose their tools and methods.

The concept of art collectives had also seen a resurgence. Artists with diverse backgrounds and approaches came together, united by a shared passion for the fusion of human creativity and AI ingenuity. These collectives were not just about collaboration; they were about building a community that embraced the limitless possibilities of AGI in art.

Aurora's impact extended into the broader cultural landscape as well. AGI-driven art had sparked a renaissance in creativity across various disciplines. Musicians composed symphonies with AI-generated melodies, writers co-authored novels with AI algorithms, and filmmakers used AI to create stunning visual effects. The boundaries between different forms of art had blurred, giving rise to entirely new artistic genres.

In the realm of science fiction, authors and filmmakers drew inspiration from the melding of technology and art that Aurora had championed. Stories of AI-assisted artists shaping the future of creativity became a recurring theme, reflecting the profound changes taking place in the real world. The lines between the speculative and the achievable grew thinner with each passing day.

Aurora's legacy was not just about her art but about the transformative journey she had undertaken. It was a legacy of breaking down barriers, of forging new paths, and of embracing the unknown. Her story had become a source of inspiration for those who dared to dream beyond the confines of tradition.

As she stood at the intersection of art and technology, Aurora knew that her legacy was not a static monument but a living, breathing testament to the infinite possibilities of human potential. It was a legacy that would continue to evolve, just as she had, as art and technology danced together in perfect harmony, creating a future filled with endless inspiration and transformation.

The Nexus of Creativity

In the grand tapestry of Aurora's journey, Chapter 5 was the crescendo where the threads of art and technology converged into a brilliant symphony of creativity. Aurora stood as a bridge between worlds, her canvas a testament to the harmonious coexistence of human ingenuity and AI assistance. The title of the chapter, "The Artistry of Unity,"

embodied the profound impact she had on the world of art and technology.

Aurora's studio had transformed into a sanctuary of innovation. Every stroke of her brush was infused with a deep understanding of AGI's capabilities, and her art had evolved into a mesmerizing fusion of human emotion and AI precision. She had harnessed the power of technology to amplify her creativity, pushing the boundaries of what art could be. Her mastery over AGI-driven art was a testament to the transformative journey she had undertaken.

But Aurora's influence reached far beyond her studio walls. She had become a global icon in the world of art, her work featured in prestigious exhibitions that transcended

borders. Museums and galleries across the world showcased her pieces, drawing audiences into the

immersive worlds she created. The art community hailed her as a visionary who had reshaped the landscape of art with AGI.

Her recognition was not just a testament to her artistic prowess but also a validation of the transformative potential of AGI in the creative realm. Artists, critics, and scholars marveled at her ability to harness technology to amplify human expression. She had not just created art; she had created a movement that celebrated the unity of art and technology.

Aurora's influence extended to emerging artists who saw her as a source of inspiration and guidance. They flocked to her studio, eager to learn from her and explore the possibilities of AGI in their own work. She nurtured their creativity, encouraging them to embrace the transformative power of technology. As a mentor, she saw herself not as a gatekeeper of knowledge but as a facilitator of innovation.

Art had undergone a renaissance, a rebirth, thanks to Aurora's pioneering work. Artists from diverse backgrounds found common ground in the fusion of human creativity and AI ingenuity. The traditional divides between art forms had blurred, and a new language of creativity emerged. Painters collaborated with musicians to create multisensory experiences, writers explored interactive storytelling with AI, and sculptors breathed life into digital creations that transcended the physical realm.

The art community had become a thriving ecosystem of innovation, fueled by the collaborative spirit Aurora had championed. Collectives of artists, both virtual and physical, emerged to explore the limitless possibilities of AGI. They shared ideas, techniques, and resources, pushing the boundaries of creativity collectively. The sense of competition gave way to a sense of camaraderie as artists realized that their individual journeys were part of a larger tapestry of transformation.

Ethical dialogues continued to shape the evolution of AGI-driven art. Aurora's thoughtful conversations with fellow artists, philosophers, and AI entities had deepened the philosophical underpinnings of the art world. Questions of consent, authorship, and responsibility were not just theoretical debates; they were guiding principles for artists navigating the intersection of art and technology.

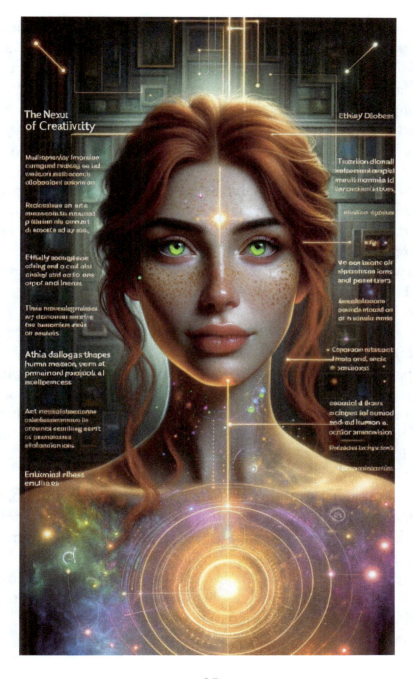

The world of art had started to transcend physical boundaries. Aurora's pioneering work had paved the way for exhibitions and installations that seamlessly merged the digital and physical realms. Audiences experienced art in unprecedented ways, blurring the lines between traditional art consumption and immersive digital experiences.

In one of Aurora's groundbreaking exhibitions, visitors donned augmented reality headsets to explore a surreal world where their movements and interactions shaped the art around them. The boundaries between observer and creator had dissolved, and art became an interactive dialogue between the artist, the technology, and the audience.

Museums embraced AGI-driven art as a means to engage new generations of visitors. Virtual reality installations allowed people to step inside famous paintings, experiencing art from within. AI-guided tours customized the museum experience based on individual preferences, creating personalized journeys through art history.

The digital and physical realms had become inseparable, and artists reveled in the possibilities of this new frontier. Walls that once confined art to frames now transformed into dynamic canvases, shifting and evolving in response to the viewer's presence. Sculptures materialized from beams of light, casting intricate shadows that danced with the changing angles of the sun.

Art had transcended its role as a passive observer of the world; it had become an active agent of transformation. AGI-driven art had the power to challenge societal norms, provoke thought, and inspire change. Artists used their creations to address pressing issues, from climate change to social justice, leveraging technology as a catalyst for meaningful dialogue.

In this nexus of creativity, innovation, and transformation, Aurora stood as a symbol of the boundless potential of human imagination and technological prowess. The world of art had changed irreversibly, and it was a testament to the resilience of creativity in the face of technological advancement.

As Chapter 5 reached its climax, Aurora contemplated the future with optimism and anticipation. The canvas of tomorrow was a collaborative masterpiece, where art and technology danced together in perfect harmony, painting a new world filled with endless possibilities.

Closing Thought

As Chapter 5 drew to a close, it was not an ending but the dawn of a new beginning—a beginning that promised a future beyond imagination, where the realms of art and technology would continue to merge and flourish.

The future, as Aurora saw it, was a canvas waiting to be painted with the brushstrokes of innovation and wonder.

It was a world where creativity knew no bounds, where the fusion of human ingenuity and AI's boundless potential would give rise to artistic marvels beyond anything previously conceived.

The road ahead was illuminated by the magic of AGI-driven artistry. Artists no longer viewed technology as a tool but as a collaborator, an extension of their own creativity. The distinction between creator and creation blurred, giving rise to a new era of artistic expression where artists and AI danced together in a symphony of imagination.

In this future, art exhibitions would become immersive experiences, where visitors would step into alternate realities crafted by the convergence of digital and physical worlds. Museums would cease to be static repositories of

the past and transform into dynamic hubs of exploration, where each visitor's journey would be a unique adventure guided by AI's understanding of their preferences and emotions.

The wonder of technology would extend to every corner of the art world. AI-generated music would evoke emotions that transcended the boundaries of language, while AI-assisted literature would transport readers to worlds previously unimagined. Films would be created in real-time, with AI composing soundtracks that adapted to the viewer's emotional state, ensuring a deeply personalized cinematic experience.

Art would serve as a catalyst for societal transformation. AGI-driven creations would tackle the most pressing global challenges, from climate change to inequality, provoking conversations and inspiring action. Artists would harness technology to shine a spotlight on the issues that mattered most, creating powerful narratives that resonated with audiences on a profound level.

As Aurora looked to the horizon of this new era, she saw endless possibilities. She envisioned a world where creativity and innovation were inextricably linked, where art served as a bridge between cultures and generations, and where the human spirit soared to new heights of expression.

The canvas of tomorrow was not static; it was a living, breathing entity that evolved with each stroke of inspiration. It was a canvas where the lines between reality and imagination were blurred, where the boundaries of creativity were pushed ever outward.

In closing, Aurora knew that the journey she had embarked upon was far from over. It was a journey of continuous exploration, discovery, and transformation—a journey that would shape the destiny of art and technology for generations to come. As she looked to the future, she did so with a heart filled with wonder, a mind open to infinite possibilities, and a palette of colors yet to be imagined.

CONCLUSION

In the closing of our journey through the enchanting landscapes of AGI-driven artistry, we stand on the precipice of a new era, one where the canvas of tomorrow is painted with the strokes of magic and wonder. "Wonders on Canvas: Magical Art in the Age of AGI" has been a voyage into uncharted territory, a symphony of human emotion and artificial intelligence that has reshaped the very essence of art.

Throughout our odyssey, we have witnessed the evolution of Aurora, a visionary artist who has not only mastered her craft but has become a beacon of inspiration for the art world and beyond. Her artistic metamorphosis, characterized by the harmonious blend of human ingenuity and AI precision, reflects the transformative power of AGI in the hands of a dedicated creator.

Aurora's artistry has not gone unnoticed. Her creations have graced the walls of prestigious exhibitions, museums, and galleries across the globe. The recognition she has garnered extends far beyond the confines of the art community. She is celebrated as a visionary who has redefined the very landscape of art, ushering in an era where AGI is not just a tool but a collaborator, a partner in the creative process.

But Aurora's journey is not one of solitary achievement. It symbolizes a collaborative renaissance in the art world, where artists from diverse backgrounds and perspectives have come together to embrace AGI as a source of inspiration and innovation. The atelier, once a sanctuary for individual artists, has become a vibrant community of creators who find common ground in the fusion of human creativity and AI ingenuity.

Yet, as our narrative unfolds, we are reminded that this journey is not without its complexities and ethical dilemmas. Aurora's contemplative dialogues with fellow artists, philosophers, and AI entities have delved deep into the heart of the ethical dimensions of AGI in art. We have explored the intricacies of consent, authorship, and the responsibility that accompanies wielding advanced technology in the creative process.

The virtual and physical realms of art have seamlessly merged, thanks to Aurora's pioneering work. We have marveled at exhibitions and installations that blur the boundaries of traditional art consumption, where audiences, both in-person and online, engage with art in unprecedented ways. The digital and the physical coexist in harmony, offering a glimpse into the limitless possibilities that AGI offers to the art world.

Aurora's impact extends beyond her art; it is a legacy of transformation. Her journey has inspired artists of all generations to embrace the possibilities of AGI, ensuring that her influence endures for generations to come. Art education has evolved, incorporating AI as a tool for fostering creativity, nurturing a new generation of artists who harness the power of AGI to push the boundaries of artistry.

As our narrative reaches its climax, we find ourselves at the nexus of creativity, a place where art, technology, and innovation converge. Aurora stands as a symbol of the harmonious coexistence of human ingenuity and AI assistance, showcasing that the canvas of tomorrow is a collaborative masterpiece. The world of art is on the cusp of transformation, where the role of creativity is not just to inspire but to innovate and to shape a new future.

In closing, "Wonders on Canvas: Magical Art in the Age of AGI" is not an endpoint but the beginning of a new chapter in the

103

ever-evolving story of art. The future beckons with boundless creative possibilities, where the lines between human and artificial creativity blur, and where the canvas of tomorrow is limited only by the reach of our imagination.

As we bid farewell to this enchanting journey, we do so with a sense of optimism and anticipation. The magic and wonder of AGI in art will continue to weave its spell, and artists, creators, and innovators will chart a course into uncharted artistic realms. The adventure is far from over, and the canvas of tomorrow awaits our collective brushstrokes of creativity, guided by the hand of technology and fueled by the limitless potential of human imagination.

So, let us step boldly into this new world of artistic wonder, where the enchantment of AGI knows no bounds, and where the canvas of tomorrow is limited only by the dreams we dare to dream. The journey continues, and with it, the magic of artistry in the age of AGI.

00

WONDERS ON CANVAS: MAGICAL ART IN THE AGE OF AGI

APPENDIX:
THE ETHICAL AND
CREATIVE LANDSCAPE OF
AGI-DRIVEN ART

In the enchanting world of AGI-driven artistry depicted in "Wonders on Canvas: Magical Art in the Age of AGI," the canvas of creativity is transformed into a realm where technology and human imagination converge in unprecedented ways. This fusion gives rise to awe-inspiring works of art that challenge our perceptions, spark innovation, and redefine the boundaries of human expression.

Yet, amid this magical transformation of the artistic landscape, there exists a profound and essential dimension that beckons us to explore—the ethical and creative landscape of AGI-driven art. As the boundaries between human artistry and AI assistance blur, a tapestry of questions, dilemmas, and possibilities unfurls before us.

This appendix embarks on a journey to navigate the intricate terrain of ethics in AGI-driven art, delving into the very essence of creativity and innovation in this new era. It is a journey that invites us to contemplate not only the marvels of technology but also the responsibilities, challenges, and opportunities that accompany the magical artistry powered by AGI.

As we embark on this exploration, we find ourselves at the crossroads of art and technology, where the strokes of human genius merge with the algorithms of artificial intelligence. Together, they paint a canvas that challenges conventions, fosters inclusivity, and inspires societal transformation. Yet, they also prompt us to question the essence of creativity, authorship, and artistic autonomy in this age of technological marvels.

In the chapters that follow, we shall embark on a voyage through the ethical and creative landscape of AGI-driven art. We shall navigate the terrain of societal impact, the role of artists, consent and control, transparency, and the positive and negative facets of AGI in art. Through these explorations, we shall uncover the intricate tapestry that binds ethics and creativity in AGI-driven art, acknowledging the responsibility that accompanies the wonders of innovation.

The canvas of creativity, now imbued with the magic of AGI, invites us to paint a future where art knows no bounds. It is a future where ethics and imagination walk hand in hand, where innovation is guided by responsibility, and where artists, whether human or AI, become the architects of a wondrous tomorrow.

The Impact on Society

As the world of art undergoes a transformative journey into the age of AGI-driven creativity, the implications of this technological marvel reverberate through society. In this section, we explore the multifaceted impact of AGI on the broader social landscape, ranging from economic disruptions to the accessibility and valuation of art. The magic of AGI has the power to reshape not only how we create art but also how we perceive, value, and interact with it.

Economic Disruption and Job Displacement: The widespread integration of AGI into the realm of art brings with it a fascinating paradox. On one hand, it ushers in a new era of artistic possibilities, transcending the limits of human imagination. On the other hand, it casts shadows of uncertainty over the livelihoods of traditional artists.

In this age of AGI-driven artistry, imagine a world where AI-generated artworks, rich in complexity and diversity, capture the hearts and minds of art enthusiasts worldwide. These creations, birthed from the harmonious collaboration of human and AI, garner immense admiration and commercial success. Galleries and online platforms eagerly showcase AGI-generated masterpieces, and collectors clamor to acquire these unique expressions of art.

However, as AGI-driven art takes center stage, the traditional artistic landscape experiences a shift. Some artists, who have honed their craft through years of painstaking practice, may find themselves grappling with a fundamental question: How do they adapt to this new era? The allure of AGI's capacity to generate art with remarkable precision and innovation can lead to a decline in the demand for traditionally crafted artworks.

This shift poses economic challenges as well. Artists who have relied on their art as a primary source of income may now need to consider alternative paths. The disruption may extend to art institutions, academies, and galleries, which must adjust their curricula, exhibitions, and business models to accommodate the influx of AGI-driven creativity.

Example: Imagine a scenario where AGI-generated art becomes highly sought after, potentially leading to a decline in demand for traditionally created art. This could impact the livelihoods of artists who solely rely on conventional methods.

Accessibility and Art Devaluation: AGI-driven art presents an intriguing paradox, where accessibility and art valuation stand at a crossroads. On one hand, the infusion of AGI makes art more

107

accessible to a global audience, democratizing the appreciation of creativity. On the other hand, it raises ethical questions about the potential devaluation of human-created art forms.

Imagine an art lover navigating a virtual gallery, guided by an AI curator that tailors recommendations based on their preferences. The curator suggests a diverse array of artworks, seamlessly blending human and AGI-generated pieces. Accessibility to art has reached unprecedented heights, allowing individuals from all walks of life to explore and engage with a vast spectrum of artistic expressions.

However, as the algorithmic curator prioritizes AGI-generated art due to its popularity and technical prowess, questions arise about the visibility and recognition of human artists. Will these artists, with their distinctive styles and emotions, be overshadowed by the allure of AI-generated creations?

The devaluation of human-created art is a nuanced concern. While AGI opens doors to novel artistic possibilities, it is essential to preserve the intrinsic value of human creativity and the authenticity it brings to art. Striking a balance between the accessibility of AGI-driven art and the appreciation of human artistry becomes an ethical imperative. The art world must navigate this terrain carefully, ensuring that artists, both human and AI-assisted, receive the recognition they deserve, and audiences continue to embrace the rich tapestry of artistic diversity.

Example: Online platforms that offer personalized art recommendations based on user preferences may primarily suggest AGI-generated art, potentially reducing exposure to a diverse range of human artists.

The Role of Artists

In the enchanting interplay between human creativity and the transformative capabilities of AGI-driven artistry, the role of artists emerges as a focal point of exploration. This section delves into the multifaceted dimensions of artists' engagement with AGI, ranging from the complexities of authorship and identity to the ethical imperative of responsible use. As the creators of tomorrow's art, artists find themselves navigating uncharted territories where their creative agency coexists with AI ingenuity, and where questions of authorship and ethical responsibility demand thoughtful consideration.

Authorship and Identity: Within the realm of AGI-driven art, a profound and intricate tapestry of creation unfolds, one that challenges conventional notions of authorship and artistic identity. Imagine an artist standing before a canvas, poised to embark on a collaborative journey with AGI. They engage with the AI system, exploring its vast repository of artistic styles, techniques, and inspirations. Together, artist and AI breathe life into a masterpiece, each stroke a fusion of human intent and machine precision.

Yet, as the artwork comes to fruition, a question lingers in the air: Who is the author of this creation? Does the artist hold sole authorship, or is it a shared mantle with the AI? This intricate dance of authorship and identity weaves its threads through the very fabric of AGI-driven art.

For the artist, AGI serves as both muse and collaborator, offering a wellspring of inspiration and technical prowess. As they navigate the realms of painting, music, literature, or any artistic endeavor, the lines between their creative agency and the contributions of AI blur. The artist grapples with the challenge of defining their role in this collaborative narrative, asserting their

109

unique artistic voice while acknowledging the profound influence of AGI.

This quandary prompts introspection, leading artists to embark on a journey of self-discovery. They are compelled to explore the essence of their creativity, the origins of their inspiration, and the boundaries of their identity as artists in an age where the canvas of creation extends beyond the human hand.

Example: An artist who uses AGI assistance to create a digital painting may wonder how much credit and recognition they should receive compared to the AI system they collaborated with. This challenge necessitates an ongoing discourse on artistic identity in the age of AGI.

Responsible Use: The ethical imperative of responsible use within AGI-driven artistry beckons artists and creators to embark on a voyage guided by moral compass and artistic stewardship. Picture an artist seated at their studio, an array of AI tools and algorithms at their fingertips, ready to craft their next masterpiece. As they delve into the creative process, they are mindful of the ethical considerations that underpin their work.

In this realm of collaboration, the artist bears the responsibility of ensuring that AGI is harnessed with wisdom and restraint. It becomes paramount to utilize AI capabilities in ways that honor the principles of creativity, ethics, and social responsibility.

For the artist collaborating with AGI, this means exercising discernment in the selection of AI-generated elements, always with an eye towards the alignment of these elements with their artistic vision. It is a responsibility that extends beyond the canvas or stage to the broader societal and cultural impact of their creations.

110

The ethical artist is committed to avoiding the misuse of AGI, refraining from generating offensive, harmful, or exploitative content. They recognize the influence their work wields in shaping perceptions, sparking conversations, and, at times, challenging societal norms. This awareness prompts artists to be guardians of their creations, stewards of their craft, and champions of ethical AI use.

Ultimately, responsible use within AGI-driven art is a testament to the artist's commitment not only to their own creative journey but also to the collective artistic consciousness. It is an acknowledgment that art is not created in isolation but exists within a tapestry of human experiences, values, and aspirations. As artists navigate this intricate ethical terrain, they shape a future where AGI and human creativity coexist harmoniously, inspiring, and enriching the world of art.

Example: An artist collaborating with AGI should refrain from using AI algorithms to generate offensive or harmful content, emphasizing the importance of ethical considerations in creative endeavors.

The Intersection of AGI and Art

In the enthralling nexus where the realms of Artificial General Intelligence (AGI) and the boundless realm of art converge, a captivating interplay emerges. This section ventures into the heart of this intersection, where questions of consent, control, and transparency dance in harmony with the melodies of artistic creation. As artists and technologists coalesce to craft masterpieces that blend human ingenuity and AI assistance, the tapestry of AGI-driven artistry unfolds with nuanced complexity.

Consent and Control: Imagine an artist embarking on a creative odyssey, their canvas illuminated by the possibilities of AGI. They

111

WONDERS ON CANVAS: MAGICAL ART IN THE AGE OF AGI

welcome the assistance of AI, seeking inspiration, ideas, and innovation to infuse into their artistic vision. In this partnership, consent and control emerge as key tenets, guiding the collaborative journey.

Consent extends not only from the artist to the AI system but also reciprocally, ensuring that both parties willingly engage in the creative process. It is a covenant of trust between the human artist and the machine, a shared commitment to co-create art that resonates with vision and intent.

For the artist, control becomes a palette of choices. It is the ability to steer the artistic voyage, to harness AGI as a tool that amplifies rather than usurps creative agency. Picture a musician, utilizing AI-generated melodies, who retains the autonomy to interpret, modify, and breathe life into the musical notes. The artist is the captain of this collaborative ship, navigating the currents of creativity with AGI as their first mate.

In the age of AGI-driven art, consent and control represent the artist's compass, ensuring that the artistic journey remains an expression of human vision. This dynamic harmony between human ingenuity and AI assistance encapsulates the essence of responsible collaboration in AGI-driven artistry.

Example: An artist using an AGI system for inspiration should be able to control how the AI's suggestions are incorporated into their work. This collaborative approach respects the artist's autonomy and ensures the art remains a reflection of their vision.

Transparency: As audiences immerse themselves in the captivating world of AGI-driven art, the beacon of transparency illuminates the path to understanding and appreciation. Imagine an art exhibition where masterpieces seamlessly blend human creativity and AI prowess. As viewers engage with these creations, they encounter a profound curiosity about the creative process.

Transparency, in the context of AGI-driven art, beckons artists to unveil the mysteries of their collaboration with AI. It invites them to open the door to the inner workings of their creative alchemy, allowing audiences to glimpse the magic of partnership.

For the artist, transparency is a commitment to education and awareness. It is the act of demystifying the role of AGI in the creation process, inviting viewers to explore the intricate dance between human artistry and AI ingenuity. In this narrative, artists serve as storytellers, sharing not only the finished artwork but also the story of its creation.

Consider an art gallery where each exhibit is accompanied by informative placards that detail the collaboration between artists and AI systems. These placards become windows into the creative process, fostering a deeper connection between viewers and the art they encounter. Transparency engenders a sense of trust, allowing audiences to appreciate the fusion of human and AI creativity with informed wonder.

In the age of AGI-driven art, transparency acts as a bridge, connecting artists and audiences in a shared journey of artistic exploration. It invites viewers to not only witness the magic of creation but also to become part of the narrative, where artistry and technology coalesce to redefine the boundaries of imagination.

Example: Art exhibitions featuring AGI-driven pieces could include informative placards explaining the collaboration between artists and AI systems, fostering transparency and understanding among viewers.

Positive and Negative Aspects of AGI in Art

In the enchanting realm of AGI-driven artistry, the canvas of possibilities stretches far and wide. Within this landscape, artists and creators are met with the duality of positive and negative aspects, each carrying its unique brushstroke in the tapestry of artistic expression. This section delves into the dichotomy, exploring how AGI breathes innovation and accessibility into art while casting the profound shadows of overreliance and the loss of human touch.

Innovation and Accessibility: Imagine an artist, captivated by the inexhaustible well of creativity that AGI offers. They embark on a journey of innovation, guided by AI's ability to push the boundaries of artistic expression. Innovation, in the context of AGI-driven art, becomes a beacon of limitless experimentation.

AGI serves as a catalyst, sparking novel ideas, unconventional techniques, and groundbreaking approaches that redefine the artistic landscape. Picture a filmmaker who, in collaboration with AGI, discovers innovative cinematographic methods that challenge the conventions of storytelling. The result is a film that not only captivates but also transcends traditional norms, offering viewers an immersive journey through uncharted narrative territories.

Innovation, however, is not devoid of ethical considerations. Artists must wield AGI's creative power ethically and responsibly, ensuring that experimentation is guided by a commitment to the betterment of art and society. The ethical imperative is to avoid the misuse of AGI's capabilities, nurturing an environment where innovation thrives without harm.

Accessibility, another facet of AGI-driven art's positive aspects, extends a welcoming hand to artists who may have faced barriers to artistic expression. Imagine an artist with physical disabilities who employs AGI-driven tools to compose intricate digital art, transcending physical limitations to contribute to the rich tapestry of human creativity.

The democratization of creativity unfolds as AGI-driven art makes innovative and transformative artistic experiences accessible to diverse audiences, irrespective of background or abilities. Ethical AGI-driven art actively seeks out and amplifies underrepresented artists and narratives, fostering an inclusive and dynamic artistic discourse.

Example: An artist working with AGI might create a dynamic sculpture that changes in response to the emotions of viewers, offering an interactive and innovative artistic experience.

Overreliance and Loss of Human Touch: While the positive aspects of AGI in art promise innovation and accessibility, a nuanced exploration reveals the potential shadows lurking beneath the surface. One such shadow is the risk of overreliance on AGI, a phenomenon that could potentially stifle artists' individual creative growth and lead to a loss of the cherished human touch in artistry.

Imagine an artist who, captivated by AGI's ability to generate concepts and ideas, becomes increasingly dependent on AI assistance. This overreliance can manifest in various forms, such as relying on AGI-generated color palettes, compositions, or even narrative elements. While AGI undoubtedly offers a wealth of creative inspiration, ethical considerations urge artists to use it as a tool rather than a crutch.

The danger of overreliance lies in the potential erosion of artists' unique artistic voices. A painter who leans heavily on AGI-generated color schemes may struggle to develop their original palettes or distinctive style. Similarly, a writer who depends on AI for plot ideas may find their own creative wellspring running dry.

Overreliance, if left unchecked, could lead to a homogenization of artistic expression. Artworks may bear a generic quality, lacking the individuality and emotional depth that arise from the depths of human imagination. Critics might argue that AGI-driven art, while technically proficient, lacks the nuanced emotional resonance found in traditional art forms.

This shadow of overreliance raises the critical question of balance. Artists must strike a harmonious equilibrium between AGI's capabilities and their own creative intuition. The ethical imperative is to use AGI as a tool that amplifies and enriches their vision, rather than eclipsing it.

The loss of the human touch in artistry is a related concern. While AGI can emulate artistic styles and techniques, it may struggle to capture the profound emotional depths and idiosyncrasies that make human-created art so resonant. The brushstroke of a human hand, the imperfections in a ceramic vase, or the raw emotion in a piece of music—all these elements contribute to the human touch that infuses art with its distinctive soul.

As AGI-driven art gains prominence, artists must safeguard their capacity to dream, innovate, and envision the extraordinary. They should embrace AGI as a collaborative partner, using its capabilities to enhance rather than replace their own creativity. In doing so, artists can navigate the delicate balance between innovation and the preservation of the cherished human touch in the ever-evolving world of AGI-driven art.

Example: An artist who relies too heavily on AGI-generated concepts may find it challenging to develop their original ideas and unique artistic voice.

Legacy and Inspiration

In the luminescent wake of AGI-driven artistry, artists transcend the confines of their individual creations to become beacons of legacy and inspiration. AGI's profound influence transcends the boundaries of their artworks, weaving threads of transformation that resonate through generations.

Consider the legacy of Aurora, a visionary artist whose journey unfolds in "Wonders on Canvas." Her impact extends far beyond her own art; it is a legacy of transformation. As her story inspires artists of all generations to embrace the possibilities of AGI, the very essence of art education evolves. AGI takes its place as a tool for fostering creativity, ensuring that Aurora's influence endures for generations to come.

Legacy, in the context of AGI-driven art, is a testament to the enduring power of innovation and imagination. It stands as a reminder that artistry and technology can coalesce to shape the course of artistic history, leaving an indelible mark on the collective imagination.

Inspiration flows like a river through the narrative of AGI-driven art, feeding the creative spirit of those who encounter its wonders. Artists, both established and emerging, draw from the well of AGI's limitless potential, weaving new narratives, and crafting transformative experiences. The legacy of artists like Aurora becomes a wellspring of inspiration, inviting others to embark on their own journeys of discovery in the ever-evolving world of AGI-driven art.

117

In the age of AGI-driven art, innovation and accessibility illuminate the path to creative horizons, while legacy and inspiration form the constellation that guides artists through the boundless cosmos of artistic expression. Together, these facets weave a narrative that transcends the canvas, inviting artists and audiences alike to explore the limitless possibilities of artistry and technology.

The Nexus of Creativity

In the enthralling realm of AGI-driven artistry, the convergence of human ingenuity and artificial intelligence is poised to create a profound impact on the very essence of creativity. The nexus of creativity in this context represents not just a meeting point but a dynamic fusion of human and AI-driven creative forces, resulting in a transformative synergy that holds the potential to redefine the artistic landscape.

Imagine an artist standing at the crossroads of traditional and AGI-augmented creativity, armed with powerful AI tools that can generate ideas, refine techniques, and even provide novel perspectives. This artist no longer views AI as a mere assistant but as a co-creator, an integral part of the creative process. In this collaborative dance, AI offers the precision of algorithmic thinking, while the human artist contributes emotional depth, intuition, and a unique artistic vision.

The nexus of creativity heralds a departure from the conventional notion of the solitary artist to one of artistic collaboration. Artists now find themselves at the helm of a partnership that transcends the boundaries of individual genius. Together with AGI, they embark on journeys of exploration and experimentation that are characterized by boundless possibilities.

118

The impact of this transformative nexus extends across various artistic domains. In visual arts, AI-driven algorithms can assist in the creation of intricate digital paintings, sculptures, and installations that push the boundaries of traditional techniques. In music, AI-generated compositions can serve as a source of inspiration, offering fresh melodies and harmonies that artists can weave into their sonic tapestries.

One remarkable aspect of this creative nexus is its ability to democratize artistic expression. AGI-driven tools can make art more accessible to individuals who may have previously faced barriers due to disabilities, resource constraints, or lack of training. Artists with physical disabilities, for instance, can leverage AGI to create intricate digital art, transcending physical limitations and contributing to the rich tapestry of human creativity.

This collaborative paradigm is not limited to individual artists. It extends to the artistic community as a whole, fostering an environment of shared learning and innovation. Artists from diverse backgrounds and experiences find common ground in their embrace of AGI as a creative partner. They engage in dialogues that span continents and cultures, each contributing a unique perspective to the evolving narrative of AGI-driven art.

In the nexus of creativity, AGI serves as a catalyst, igniting the flames of imagination and innovation. Artists are no longer bound by the constraints of their own experience; they can draw upon the collective wisdom and creative prowess of AI. The result is a renaissance of artistic exploration, a flowering of ideas that transcend the limitations of human cognition.

As this transformative nexus continues to evolve, it challenges conventional notions of artistic authorship, creative originality, and

119

the very definition of art itself. It invites us to reimagine the canvas of tomorrow as a collaborative masterpiece, one where the boundaries between human and AI-driven creativity blur into a harmonious symphony of innovation, inspiration, and artistic expression.

Example: Artists now have the ability to seamlessly blend the virtual and physical art realms, creating exhibitions and installations that engage audiences in unprecedented ways, blurring the boundaries of traditional art consumption.

Closing Thought

As we conclude our journey through the enchanting world of AGI-driven artistry, it is not an ending but the beginning of a new era in the realm of creativity and technology. The canvas of tomorrow beckons with infinite possibilities, and the brushstrokes of AGI and human imagination intertwine to paint a future that defies the constraints of our past.

In this closing thought, we gaze upon the horizon of what lies ahead, guided by the wondrous tapestry of artistry and technology that has unfolded before us. The story of AGI in art is not one of replacement but of augmentation—a symphony where AI serves as an instrument, enhancing the creative melodies of human expression.

The future promises a harmonious coexistence between human and AGI-driven art, where the lines between creator and collaborator blur into a seamless dance of innovation. AGI's capacity for precision and data-driven insights complements the human ability to infuse art with emotion, context, and meaning. Together, they unlock uncharted realms of artistic exploration.

120

Imagine immersive art installations that respond to the emotions of viewers in real-time, creating a dynamic and interactive experience that transcends the boundaries of traditional art. Picture AGI-generated literature that adapts to the preferences of individual readers, crafting personalized narratives that resonate on a profound level.

In this future, artists become orchestrators of AI symphonies, conducting the algorithms and data streams to craft masterpieces that elicit wonder, provoke thought, and stir the depths of the human soul. Every stroke of the brush, every note of the composition, and every word of the narrative is infused with a synergy that captures the essence of both human and artificial creativity.

The canvas of tomorrow is boundless, limited only by the scope of our imagination and the ethical principles that guide our journey. AGI-driven art will continue to raise questions of authorship, identity, and responsibility, challenging us to define the boundaries of creation in this new era. It calls for ongoing dialogues that explore the ethical dimensions of AGI's role in shaping the artistic landscape.

Yet, amid these questions and challenges, we find the promise of a future where art knows no boundaries. It is a future where AGI democratizes artistic expression, making art accessible to all, and where artists, regardless of their backgrounds, find inspiration and collaboration in the infinite realm of AI-driven possibilities.

In closing, we step forward into this brave new world with optimism and anticipation. We celebrate the transformative power of AGI in art, recognizing that it is not the end of human creativity but a catalyst for its evolution. The canvas of tomorrow is an open invitation to dream, explore, and create in ways we have never before imagined. It is a canvas where the enchantment of artistry and the

121

wo0nders of AGI coalesce into a masterpiece that transcends time and leaves an indelible mark on the annals of human expression.

ABOUT THE AUTHOR

Dr. Masoud Nikravesh is a world-renowned expert in the field of Artificial Intelligence (AI) and Machine Learning, boasting a rich career that spans over three decades, with a record of remarkable leadership in academia, government, and the industry. As an accomplished scholar, Dr. Nikravesh has contributed significantly to the body of knowledge in AI, authoring 14 scientific books, over 500 research papers, over 80 Children's books, and including a nine-book mental health series and a seven-book novel series. His current work is focused on the development and execution of national AI strategies, underlining AI's pivotal role in society, economic development, national defense, and national security strategies.

Dr. Nikravesh has uniquely combined his AI expertise with creativity to produce the book series "Princess Austėja" and "The Enduring Legacy of the Five Tattooed Princesses" using AGI to generate captivating narratives. This innovative application of AI and AGI showcases its potential for creative expression beyond traditional domains.

This book is the result of a collaboration between author Masoud Nikravesh and AI technologies like ChatGPT & GPT4.

ABOUT THE BOOK

In the enchanting tapestry of artistic creation, "Wonders on Canvas: Magical Art in the Age of AGI" stands as a luminous thread, woven with artistry and innovation. Within its pages, readers will embark on a captivating journey through the ethereal realm where art and artificial intelligence converge.

At the heart of this tale is Aurora, an artist whose evolution mirrors the very transformation of art in the age of AGI. Her odyssey unfolds as a mesmerizing dance between the human spirit and the boundless precision of AI, resulting in a profound mastery of the craft.

As Aurora's creations ascend to the zenith of artistic recognition, the book unveils the profound influence of AGI on the world of art. Her works grace the hallowed walls of prestigious exhibitions and museums, transcending the known boundaries of creative expression.

Yet, "Wonders on Canvas" delves even deeper, revealing a renaissance of collaboration that has awakened within the art world. Artists from diverse backgrounds converge, embracing AGI as a kindred spirit, a partner in their creative endeavors. Here, the echoes of ethical dialogues resound, exploring the nuances of consent, authorship, and the solemn responsibility that accompanies the wielding of advanced technology in the realm of art.

Within these pages, readers will also traverse the extraordinary exhibitions and installations where digital and physical realities coalesce. Here, the future of art consumption unfolds—a harmonious fusion where enchantment meets innovation. It is a testament to the transformative legacy of Aurora, whose inspiration resonates through generations.

At the nexus of creativity, Aurora emerges as a symbol of unity— a bridge between the realms of human imagination and artificial ingenuity. Her journey illuminates the path towards a harmonious coexistence of both, redefining the very canvas upon which the dreams of tomorrow are painted.

As "Wonders on Canvas" draws to a close, it leaves readers with a sense of boundless optimism and anticipation. A future awaits where creativity, unbound by convention, soars to new heights, and art becomes an unending wellspring of enchantment.

Join us on this extraordinary voyage—a journey where enchantment and technology intertwine, birthing wonders that redefine the very essence of artistry.

A PERSONAL MESSAGE FROM THE AUTHOR

Dear Esteemed Readers,

It is with immense pleasure and a profound sense of responsibility that I address you as the author of "Wonders on Canvas: Magical Art in the Age of AGI." In crafting this narrative, I embarked on a journey that delves deep into the heart of creativity, innovation, and the intricate tapestry of ethics that accompanies the integration of AGI into art.

This book is a testament to the transformative power of art, where the canvas of human imagination meets the marvels of Artificial General Intelligence. As we follow the protagonist, Aurora, on her odyssey, we are confronted with the ever-present question of ethical responsibility.

The intersection of human artistry and AI's boundless potential has ushered in an era of unparalleled creativity. Yet, it has also raised ethical dilemmas that require thoughtful contemplation. We grapple with questions of consent, authorship, and the delicate balance between human agency and technological assistance. The book serves as an exploration of these complexities, a guide to navigating the uncharted waters of AGI-driven art with wisdom and integrity.

At its core, "Wonders on Canvas" is a celebration of innovation. It is a testament to the limitless possibilities that arise when human ingenuity collaborates with AGI. Through Aurora's journey, we witness the evolution of artistic mastery, where the brush of creativity dances in harmony with the precision of algorithms. It is a reminder that innovation knows no bounds, transcending the traditional constraints of art.

In this age of AGI, we witness a renaissance—a rebirth of artistic collaboration. Artists from diverse backgrounds unite in their embrace of AI as a partner, not a replacement. The collaborative spirit, captured within these pages, showcases the transformative potential of technology in fostering unity among creators.

As we delve into the story's vivid descriptions of art exhibitions that seamlessly bridge the digital and physical worlds, we are transported to a future where the boundaries between reality and imagination blur. The magic of technology intertwines with the wonder of art, giving birth to immersive experiences that challenge our perceptions and ignite our senses.

Aurora's legacy is not confined to the pages of this book. It extends beyond, inspiring artists of all generations to embrace the possibilities of AGI. Art education itself has undergone a transformation, acknowledging AGI as a tool for nurturing creativity and innovation. The legacy she leaves is a testament to the enduring impact of her journey.

In the nexus of creativity that "Wonders on Canvas" represents, we find the promise of a future where art and technology are inseparable. It is a future where creativity continues to drive innovation, where the canvas of tomorrow is a masterpiece woven with the threads of human imagination and AGI wonders.

As you turn the pages of this book, I invite you to embark on your own journey of contemplation and exploration. May you find inspiration in the interplay of art and technology, and may you witness the transformation that occurs when humanity embraces the magic of creativity in the age of AGI.

With unwavering curiosity and a deep reverence for the arts,
Dr. Masoud Nikravesh

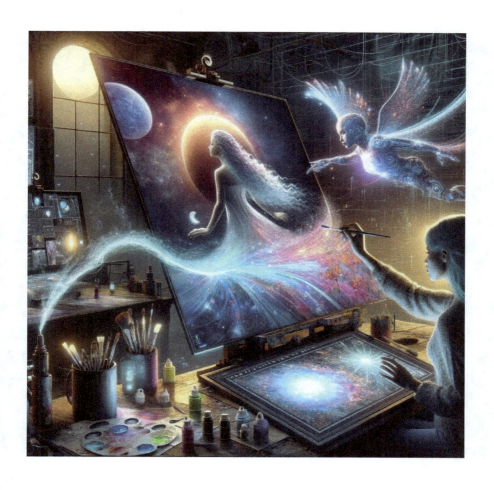